The Lost Railways of Yorkshire's Eas
Neil Burgess

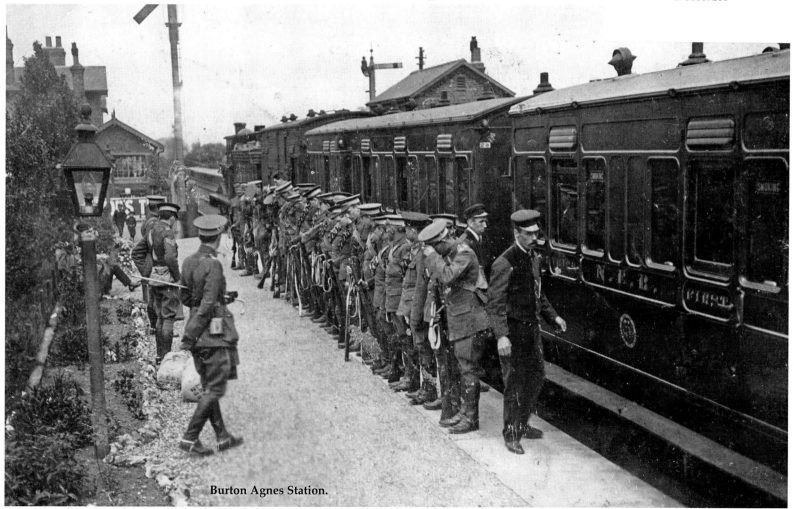

Burton Agnes Station.

Holme Station.

© Neil Burgess, 2011
First published in the United Kingdom, 2011,
by Stenlake Publishing Ltd.
www.stenlake.co.uk
ISBN 9781840335521

Printed by
Blissetts, Roslin Road, Acton, W3 8DH

Acknowledgements

I am again most grateful to my friend and fellow railway historian Richard Morton for his painstaking proof reading of the text of this book. As a Yorkshireman, he has a particular interest in the subject and I have gained much from his insights. The publishers wish to thank the following for contributing photographs: John Alsop for the front cover, pages 1, 2, 4, 6, 7, 9, 11, 12, 13, 14, 15, 16, 20 (both), 21, 22, 23, 26, 29, 30, 31, 32, 33, 34, 37, 38, 41 (both), 42, 43, 44, 45, 46 (both), 47, 48 and the inside back cover; and Richard Casserley for the inside front cover, pages 5, 8, 10, 17, 18, 19, 24, 25, 27, 28, 36, 39, 40 and the back cover.

Introduction

Of the three historic divisions of Yorkshire, the East Riding, historically bounded by the rivers Ouse and Derwent, is probably the least known, particularly to those living in other parts of the country. It has neither the industrial sprawl and population of the West Riding, nor the high rugged moorland of the North; but in the Wolds it has rolling limestone landscapes as attractive as any in England, a low-lying expanse of country along the coastal hinterland of Holderness, including the ever-shifting Spurn Head, and attractive old towns like Driffield, Market Weighton and Beverley, the latter a garrison town with a fine mediaeval minster. The city of Kingston-upon-Hull is by far the largest settlement in the East Riding and remains an important trading and ferry port with northern Europe.

Railways reached Hull in 1840, by way of Selby. The Leeds & Selby Railway had initially been proposed in 1824, at the same time as the Liverpool & Manchester, foreseeing a direct railway link between the west and east coasts of England. After initial difficulties were overcome, the company gained parliamentary consent for the route in 1830 and it opened to passengers on 22 September 1834. In July of the same year a proposal had been made for a line between Hull and Selby and a company of that name was authorised to construct a railway by an Act of 21 June 1836. The route opened from 1 July 1840.

Railways in the 1840s were dominated by the person of George Hudson, a draper from York who made – and later lost – a fortune through railway promotion. The York & North Midland Railway was one of the companies under his control and it went on to construct several lines through and just beyond the East Riding. Hudson was deeply antagonistic to the Manchester & Leeds Railway, which later formed the basis of the Lancashire & Yorkshire and which reached Goole in 1848. Four years earlier, the Hull & Selby had entered into an alliance with the Manchester & Leeds which might have led eventually to amalgamation, so Hudson countered this perceived threat by arranging for the York & North Midland to lease the Hull & Selby, shareholders voting against the advice of their directors to secure it. Thus it was that in 1854, several years after Hudson's disgrace and exile, the York & North Midland joined with other companies to form the North Eastern Railway, which established an effective monopoly over the railways of the East Riding.

The North Eastern was, or certainly became, not only one of Britain's most prosperous railway companies but also one of the most progressive, advocating electrification of its portion of the East Coast main line in the 1920s, fully seventy years before the project was eventually undertaken by British Rail. It dominated railway communication east of the Pennines from Hull to Berwick-on-Tweed, though it conceded running powers to both the Lancashire & Yorkshire and the London & North Western and they operated services of express passenger trains between Liverpool and Hull and Liverpool and York well into the twentieth century. Even so, there were those during the Victorian age who resented the North Eastern's pre-eminence and in the East Riding this led to the promotion of one of the few companies intended to be large enough to threaten it. The Hull & Barnsley was an impressively well-engineered line linking the West Riding to Hull; however, it arrived too late on the scene to achieve what its promoters hoped for.

Apart from Hull and its thriving port there was little industry in the East Riding beyond agriculture and some quarrying. The lines built radiating out from Hull therefore tended to be secondary routes serving the low-lying reaches of Holderness or the attractive villages and small towns dotted around the Wolds. As this account indicates, most have long gone, though the line from Hull to Scarborough is still open, including the historic train sheds at Beverley and Filey, both designed by G.T. Andrews for the York & North Midland. Even Hull itself has undergone changes of fortune over the years, losing its direct connections to the East Coast main line and London during the 1970s, though this situation has since been rectified due to the creation of Hull Trains. The holiday destinations of Bridlington and Filey, the latter renowned for its holiday camp during the post-war period, provide significant traffic over the line through Beverley from Hull, even though the railway is at a distance from the Holderness resorts of Hornsea and Withernsea since their respective branches from Hull closed.

Railways in the East Riding today mirror many of the trends observable throughout the country. The surviving routes tend to be the oldest, in this case along the north shore of the Humber through Goole to Doncaster and Leeds, and through Beverley to Bridlington. Later arrivals, large and small, tend to have gone. Much of the surviving freight traffic is in bulk and long-distance and the mainstay of the railways' revenue is now passenger traffic. Both show an encouraging upward trend. Elsewhere, those who know their history can find traces of lines long disappeared, weaving their way through a rural landscape which has scarcely changed since the villages along the branch lines still had a train service.

Beverley — York *

Passenger service withdrawn	29 November 1965
Distance	33 ¾ miles
Company	York & North Midland Railway

Stations closed	*Date of closure*
Cherry Burton	5 January 1959
Kipling Cotes	29 November 1965
Market Weighton	29 November 1965
Londesborough **	29 November 1965
Nunburnholme ***	1 April 1951

Stations closed	*Date of closure*
Pocklington	29 November 1965
Fangfoss	5 January 1959
Stamford Bridge	29 November 1965

* Closed passenger stations on this line that were in the North Riding were Holtby, Warthill and Earswick.
** Originally named Shipton until January 1867.
*** Originally named Burnby until 1 January 1873.

Cherry Burton Station.

Locomotive No. 62367 entering Market Weighton with a train from Driffield, 2 June 1957.

One of the more notorious figures in the early years of railway building and development was George Hudson, a financier who started life as a draper in the city of York and managed to acquire a fortune by promoting railways. Hudson was one of those who realised early on that the future of railways lay not with a host of small, local undertakings but with large companies which could provide the capital and expertise to build, maintain and develop the railway system. He was also dishonest and in time his financial misdemeanours came to light, resulting in his downfall and ruin. The Midland Railway was his great creation which long outlasted him, but the York & North Midland, which eventually became a constituent of the North Eastern Railway, was also his handiwork.

The York & North Midland promoted a line from York to Beverley in 1846 and it opened as far as Market Weighton from 4 October the following year. The route was originally threatened by competition from canals, but the Y&NMR was able to buy them out in the year the line opened. This section of railway was very much George Hudson's local line, passing by his home at Londesborough Park, just outside of Market Weighton, and a private station of that name was built for his convenience half a mile from the public station at Londesborough, a tree-lined avenue linking the house with the station. Hudson had bought Londesborough and the 12,000 acres of land which formed its park in order to prevent an ally of the Manchester & Leeds Railway – the genesis of the Lancashire & Yorkshire – from building a rival line between Market Weighton and Hull, but he had little opportunity to enjoy it since he fell from grace in 1849 after an enquiry uncovered his malpractice. He lived in obscurity until his death in 1871.

A wave of financial speculation in railways, known to history as the 'Railway Mania', which Hudson had done much to encourage by his promotions, engulfed the late 1840s, but like all such 'bubbles' it eventually burst, bringing profit to some but ruin to many. Railway schemes which had seemed financial certainties during the Mania collapsed with it and many lines were left without capital to complete them. The section of the Beverley line beyond Market Weighton was one, and it remained unfinished until 1865 and then only as a single-track route. Twenty-four years later, and 43 after being authorised, it was finally doubled in 1889, by which time the York & North Midland had given way to the North Eastern.

Pocklington Station.

The line as far as Market Weighton was built through relatively easy country, but at Stamford Bridge, near where Harold Godwinson, last Saxon king of England, had defeated the Danes in 1066, it crossed the valley of the River Derwent. The line was carried over the river on a large and impressive brick viaduct with ten arches on the York side and five opposite, the water itself being spanned by a graceful cast-iron central section. Even beyond Market Weighton the passage through the Wolds was without severe gradients, the steepest being just 1 in 151.

For most of its life the route's easy gradients made it a busy cross-country line passing through a predominantly agricultural area; there was some seasonal and holiday traffic towards the east coast in the summer. Such lines were considered ripe for economies as the twentieth century wore on and Warthill gained a small place in British railway history in 1953 by becoming the site of the first ever public level crossing with lifting barriers rather than conventional gates. At the time barriers were a feature of crossings in Europe, but in the intervening half century they have become predominant, though not yet universal, in Britain.

Developments at Warthill were to be a harbinger of more ambitious changes. In 1960 plans were announced to single the entire route, leaving passing loops controlled by signal boxes at Pocklington and Market Weighton. Seven other boxes were to be closed and nineteen level crossings converted for working with automatic barriers. Signalling of the whole route was to be centralised at York and it was intended to apply the same method of operation to other East Riding lines, including the Holderness branches to Hornsea and Withernsea (see separate sections). Preliminary work was undertaken before the scheme was halted for reassessment in early 1962 and was soon abandoned altogether. The reassessment seems to have been prompted by the forthcoming report *Re-shaping Britain's Railways*, known to history as the Beeching Report after its author, which appeared in 1963. This recommended closure of the entire route, which eventually occurred, despite public protest, from 27 November 1965.

Beverley — York

Driffield — Malton

Passenger service withdrawn	5 June 1950
Distance	20 miles
Company	Malton & Driffield Railway

Stations closed	*Date of closure*
Garton	5 June 1950
Wetwang	5 June 1950

Stations closed	*Date of closure*
Sledmere & Fimber	5 June 1950
Burdale	5 June 1950
Wharram	5 June 1950
North Grimston	5 June 1950
Settrington	5 June 1950

Wetwang Station.

Though this line was a rural byway, it had originally been promoted as part of an independent main line linking Hull with the northeast and opened for traffic on 19 May 1853. The engineer for the route was John Birkinshaw, a former pupil of Robert Stephenson; he in turn employed Alfred Lamerte Dickens, younger brother of the great Victorian novelist, as an assistant and supervisor of the works, so the Malton & Driffield was well connected to the great figures of the first half of the nineteenth century.

Driffield — Malton

Changing tablets at Wharram Station, 10 June 1934.

The company's independence was short lived and it was absorbed into the North Eastern Railway in 1854, possibly much to the relief of its promoters; building a railway was one thing, but operating it in perpetuity was quite another.

Driffield — Malton

North Grimston Station, 2 June 1957.

The line was single track throughout, burrowing through the Wolds by means of a 1,746-yard tunnel between Wharram and Burdale, and provided a means of communication with the wider world for the villages along its route. Unsurprisingly, however useful this might have been it proved insufficient to sustain the line up to its centenary and in 1950 passenger services ceased. In its later years quarries near Burdale provided a considerable traffic in limestone for the blast furnaces of Teesside and in chalk, but this ceased in 1958, with general goods lingering on until final closure in October of the same year. Several of the station buildings remain, but many of the earthworks have long disappeared.

Driffield — Malton

A curious postscript to the story of the line is the extension beyond Driffield to Frodingham Bridge. Five miles of single line were included in the original proposals, but in the event the line was never built. Even so, Frodingham Bridge managed to appear on North Eastern Railway maps over the years as terminus of two unbuilt light railways, the North Holderness Light Railway and the Bridlington & North Frodingham Light Railway, lost railways in more ways than one!

Hull — Cudworth *

Passenger service withdrawn	See text	*Stations closed*	*Date of closure*
Distance	53 miles	Sandholme	1 August 1955
Company	Hull & Barnsley Railway	North Eastrington Halt	1 August 1955
		South Howden	1 August 1955
Stations closed	*Date of closure*	Barmby	1 January 1932
Hull Cannon Street	14 July 1924		
Hull Beverley Road	14 July 1924	* Closed passenger stations on this line that were in the West Riding were	
Springhead Halt **	1 August 1955	Drax, Carlton Towers, Kirk Smeaton, Upton & North Elmsall,	
Willerby & Kirk Ella	1 August 1955	Hemsworth & South Kirkby and Cudworth.	
Little Weighton	1 August 1955	** Built by LNER.	
South Cave	1 August 1955	*** Originally named Newport; renamed Newport (Yorks) in September	
North Cave	1 August 1955	1921 and as Wallingfen on 1 July 1923.	
Wallingfen ***	1 August 1955		

Hull & Barnsley Railway locomotive No. 9 at Hull Cannon Street Station. This was among the company's first batch of twelve engines, designed by William Kirtley and built in 1884. They were scrapped in 1922.

Hull — Cudworth

Willerby & Kirk Ella Station.

From its arrival in the city the North Eastern Railway had laid claim to Hull, but by doing so raised the spectre of monopoly, which so vexed Victorian politicians and businessmen. Local traders chafed at the North Eastern, believing it to be charging dearly for poor service, and during the late 1870s their concerns, supported by the city corporation, prompted a scheme to construct an alternative connection between the West Riding and the city. Authorised by an act of Parliament in 1880, the Hull, Barnsley & West Riding Junction Railway & Dock Company – more commonly known as the Hull & Barnsley Railway, a title it came to adopt for itself – opened its line to Hull on 27 July 1885, terminating at Cannon Street. A fortnight before, on 16 July, the company had also opened the new Alexandra Dock, so ensuring unimpeded access to the Humber estuary and the North Sea.

Hull — Cudworth

Little Weighton Station.

The new railway certainly sought to convince potential users of its solidity and sense of purpose. The North Eastern had followed the relatively easy approach to Hull along the north bank of the Humber, so the Hull & Barnsley was obliged to take a route further inland, crossing the southern extremity of the Wolds with a line which included six or so miles in each direction at gradients between 1 in 100 and 1 in 150 up to a summit just west of Little Weighton Station. There were several tunnels, of which Drewton, at 1 mile 354 yards, was the longest; and also a spectacular cutting, three-quarters of a mile long and nearly 90 feet deep, through the chalk at Little Weighton. The River Ouse was crossed near Drax on an impressive swing bridge in order to preserve the navigation on the river. Even the small stations were substantial structures, which have mostly lasted far longer in private ownership than they ever did in railway service.

Like many later arrivals on the national network, the Hull & Barnsley was at a disadvantage from the first, though it made every effort to compete with the North Eastern. During the early years of the twentieth century it promoted express passenger services to Sheffield, but these did not prosper. The relatively sparse population west of Hull meant local passenger services were never likely to thrive either; so goods traffic was, and remained, the mainstay of the Hull & Barnsley, which promoted itself as the 'Continental Route via Hull', even having the slogan painted onto its wagons, a decidedly unusual step for a British railway company. However, in the year before the 1923 Grouping it was absorbed by its old rival and thereafter was doomed to play a secondary role in the new London & North Eastern Railway network. Cannon Street terminus closed in 1924, trains being rerouted into the North Eastern's Paragon Station.

Hull — Cudworth

During the 1920s both the LNER and the LMS experimented with Sentinel geared steam railcars as a potentially cheaper way of working secondary lines than conventional locomotives and coaches. The Hull & Barnsley was one such route, but the railcars could not reverse the line's losses on passenger operations. The great depression of 1929 did nothing to help and the western end of the system, beyond South Howden, lost its passenger service three years later. The majority of the system in the East Riding held onto its passenger services until 1955, most being worked by push-pull trains which the railway companies had concluded offered greater flexibility than the railcars.

The LNER was probably the British railway company most badly affected by the Depression, but goods traffic remained sufficient to ensure the line's survival until 29 November 1958, when through traffic finished (although the pick-up goods to Carlton Towers continued until 6 April 1959). The staffs at stations beyond South Howden were effectively working on a ghost railway for five months. These closures left the North Eastern line to again become the main way into Hull, though a short section of the Hull & Barnsley remains in the city to give access to the docks. Given that coal was very much the foundation of the company's fortunes, it is appropriate that the only other surviving section is the short connection to the coal-fired Drax Power Station, reopened in 1972.

Hull — Hornsea

Passenger service withdrawn	19 October 1964	*Stations closed*	*Date of closure*
Distance	15 ½ miles	Ellerby (2nd station) **	19 October 1964
Company	Hull & Hornsea Railway	Ellerby (1st station)	1 July 1902
		Whitedale	19 October 1964
Stations closed	*Date of closure*	Sigglesthorne	19 October 1964
Hull Botanic Gardens	19 October 1964	Wassand ***	21 September 1953
Stepney	19 October 1964	Hornsea Bridge	19 October 1964
Sculcoates	9 June 1912	Hornsea Town	19 October 1964
Wilmington (1st station)	9 June 1912		
Wilmington (2nd station) *	19 October 1964	* This replaced the first station.	
Sutton-on-Hull	19 October 1964	** Named as Marton until 1 August 1864 and as Burton Constable until	
Swine	19 October 1964	1 January 1922 when it replaced the first Ellerby Station.	
Skirlaugh	6 May 1957	*** Named Goxhill until 1 October 1904.	

Hull Botanic Gardens Station.

Hull Botanic Gardens Station, 31 August 1956.

This, the second of the lines from Hull into Holderness, was promoted in 1861, authorised on 30 June 1862 and opened on 28 March 1864, being worked from the first by the North Eastern, on which it was dependent for its access to Hull. Sharing an entry to Hull with the Withernsea line, the Hull & Hornsea effectively ended at Wilmington because the Railway Inspectorate of the Board of Trade declined to authorise the use of the junction with the York & North Midland Railway. With the improvement of the Victoria Dock branch in July 1864 (see entry on the Hull & Holderness Railway) trains started and terminated at Paragon, which was exactly what had originally been intended.

Hull — Hornsea

Stepney Station, 31 August 1956.

Hull — Hornsea

The Hornsea company was in financial difficulties from the outset, the line costing almost twice as much to build as had been estimated; disgruntled creditors actually seized and sold some of the line's furnishings and fittings in order to recoup their debts. As with the Withernsea company, only the resources of the North Eastern offered a way out of the line's difficulties and it was formally absorbed by its greater neighbour on 16 July 1866.

Hull — Hornsea

Sutton-on-Hull Station, *c.*1916.

Sutton-on-Hull Station.

Hull — Hornsea

Both the Holderness lines had similar train services, of around ten trains each way daily in 1910. Market day traffic added variety to the regular services, as did excursions at holiday times. Both lines had relatively high operating costs because crossing the flat countryside meant frequent level crossings over roadways, each requiring a signal box, or at least a crossing keeper, to look after them. In steam days there was little which could be done about this, but during the 1950s the advent of multiple-unit diesel railcars offered an opportunity to reduced train costs.

Whitedale Station.

The arrival of the new trains in 1959 led to the withdrawal of staff from all the stations on both lines, except Withernsea, Hornsea Town and Hornsea Bridge, from 4 January 1960; henceforth tickets could be issued on the train by the guard. The original intention was to follow this by replacing the conventional level crossings with automatic lifting barriers controlled by continuous track-circuiting, which could also be used to actuate the signals – much the same as is done on many lines today.

Hull — Hornsea

Hull — Hornsea

Hornsea Bridge Station, 31 August 1956.

Hull — Hornsea

Locomotive No. 77000 with the 10.58 a.m. train to Hull at Hornsea Town Station, 31 August 1956.

But British Railways was reluctant to make the capital investment needed to carry out the work and the subsequent operating losses were used to justify closure to passengers from 17 October 1964. Goods traffic lasted only another seven months, though the portions of the lines within the urban areas of Hull survived for a number of years beyond this. Since closure the Hornsea line has been converted to a cycle way from Wilmington and Hornsea Town Station has been incorporated into a housing development. Several sections of the Withernsea line have also become cycle ways.

Hull — Hornsea

Hull — Withernsea

Passenger service withdrawn	19 October 1964	*Stations closed*	*Date of closure*
Distance	20 ¾ miles *	Hedon	19 October 1964
Company	Hull & Holderness Railway	Rye Hill & Burstwick	19 October 1964
		Keyingham	19 October 1964
		Ottringham	19 October 1964
Stations closed	*Date of closure*	Winestead	1 July 1904
Hull Victoria Dock	1 June 1864	Patrington	19 October 1964
Hull Botanic Gardens	19 October 1964	Withernsea	19 October 1964
Stepney	19 October 1964		
Sculcoates	9 June 1912	* Some sources quote 18 miles, possibly the original distance (see text).	
Southcoates	19 October 1964		
Marfleet	19 October 1964		

Hedon Station.

Hull — Withernsea

Many shorter routes were originally developed by local companies out of a desire to connect a locality to the national railway network. On completion they were often either worked from the outset by a larger neighbour, generally the one with which their services connected, or else operated independently for a time only to be taken over later. The lines to Withernsea and Hornsea were both local undertakings absorbed after several years by the North Eastern Railway.

Hull — Withernsea

Ottringham Station, 31 August 1956.

The line to Withernsea was the first to penetrate Holderness, the area of rural land to the east of Hull. Obtaining its act of Parliament in 1853, the line was relatively easy to build over the level and low-lying country and it was opened on 24 June the following year. The major engineering works were few, principally the swing bridge over the River Hull at Sculcoates, still in existence and known as Wilmington Bridge. The line ran into a terminus at Hull Victoria Dock, which it shared with the York & North Midland Railway, though originally it had been envisaged that a connection might be built to Paragon Station, for which running powers had been granted although were never used. The York & North Midland had opened its Victoria Dock branch in May 1853 and in its first year of operation tried a speculative passenger service from Manor House to Victoria Dock. It proved unsuccessful and was abandoned in November of the following year.

Hull — Withernsea

The Hull & Holderness pursued a course of doughty independence until 1860, but it had by then become clear that the resources of its larger neighbour were needed if the line was to receive adequate financial support. Taking over operation in 1860, the North Eastern absorbed the Hull & Holderness completely from 17 July 1862. On doing so it set to work to improve the line, the Hull end being doubled, but the swing bridge at Sculcoates remained with the two running lines interlaced; effectively making that a single-track section, even though the majority of the route was double track. Victoria Dock Station closed in 1864, services being diverted to Paragon – which added two miles or so to the distance from Withernsea. This alteration brought about the paradoxical situation of Withernsea trains leaving Hull westwards, effectively reversing direction as they travelled round the city.

During the twentieth century the North Eastern continued doubling the line, replacing the Sculcoates bridge with one carrying double track in 1907 although the Hedon–Rye Hill and Ottringham–Winestead sections were never doubled. The line, and its neighbour to Hornsea (see separate section) benefited from the popularity of Holderness as a holiday destination for day visitors and longer stays, but eventually succumbed to closure in 1964.

Hull — Withernsea

Layerthorpe — Cliff Common

Passenger service withdrawn	1 September 1926	*Stations closed*	*Date of closure*
Distance	16 miles	Dunnington for Kexby	1 September 1926
Company	Derwent Valley Light Railway	Elvington	1 September 1926
		Wheldrake	1 September 1926
Stations closed	*Date of closure*	Cottingwith	1 September 1926
Layerthorpe	1 September 1926	Thorganby	1 September 1926
Osbaldwick	1 March 1915	Skipwith & North Duffield	1 September 1926
Murton Lane	1 September 1926	Cliff Common	1 September 1926
Dunnington halt	1 September 1926		

Elvington Station on the day of the opening of the Derwent Valley Light Railway, 19 July 1913.

Wheldrake Station.

OPENING DERWENT VALLEY LIGHT RAILWAY 19 JULY 1913

The passing of the Light Railways Act by Parliament in 1896 opened up the possibility of constructing railways, to either standard or narrow gauge, to serve remote or sparsely-populated areas of the country where a fully engineered line would not be viable. Local authorities were permitted to make grants or loans towards the cost of construction and a Treasury grant was also provided. This was an approach which had been tried in rural Ireland before being applied to the rest of Britain and was responsible for much of the network of mainly narrow gauge lines in that country.

In the East Riding the agricultural hinterland of York was an area where the need to transport produce quickly and effectively to markets all over Britain led to discussions about constructing a light railway within a few years of the passage of the 1896 act. Though the rural district councils of Riccall and Escrick had declared their support for such a project in 1898, the line was not actually built until 1912, financed largely by local landowners, and opened to traffic on 21 July 1913. It ran from Layerthorpe, on the North Eastern Railway's Foss Island goods line in York to Cliff Common on the Selby–Market Weighton line, more or less parallel to the River Derwent, but a mile or so to the west of it, sixteen miles in all.

Layerthorpe — Cliff Common

The company, which managed to retain its independence throughout its existence despite the grouping of 1923 and nationalisation in 1948, sought to operate the line as economically as possible, hiring locomotives from the North Eastern to work the trains rather than buying its own. In May 1924 it attempted to economise still further by buying two Ford 3-ton road lorries, having bus bodies fitted to them by C.H. Roe Ltd of Leeds and converting them to run on rails as improvised railcars at a total cost of £1,070, a not inconsiderable sum for the time. The passenger service seems always to have been minimal, the original service of four trains a day each way in 1913 being reduced to three a day each way on weekdays and four each way on Saturdays by 1922. A note in the July 1922 timetable relating to the midday train on Saturday reveals that 'For parties of 10 or more, arrangements will be made to run beyond Wheldrake', suggesting that the company saw no point in being too optimistic about passenger numbers; the last Saturday train terminated at Wheldrake however many people it carried. Four years later even the railcars seemed to have done all they could and passenger services were terminated. W.T.D. Grundy, the general manager, advertised the railcars for sale and they were bought by the County Donegal Railway in Ireland, which rebuilt them extensively in order to run them on the three-foot gauge. The DVLR was paid £480 for the two railcars and might have got less had not the redoubtable Colonel Holman Fred Stephens wanted them for the East Kent Railway; they even threw in a new spare engine, gearbox and magneto to seal the sale. It cost the CDR £128 11s 8d to rebuild them, numbering them 2 and 3 in their railcar fleet. They remained working until 1934, but their new owners learned valuable lessons from them which they applied in developing railcar working over the Donegal system.

The DVLR thus spent most of its existence as a goods line, usually continuing the tradition of hiring locomotives from the North Eastern and later the LNER and British Railways; in later days a 204 hp diesel shunter was the favoured motive power. Nevertheless, for two years from 1925 the company owned a Sentinel vertical-boilered geared steam locomotive which it bought new from the builders in Shrewsbury. It was a type examples of which both the LMS and LNER subsequently bought and it is said that because of their interest the two companies allowed the engine to be delivered to York free of charge. However the engine was unable to persuade the company that it was not more economical to hire motive power and it was sold in 1927.

Cliff Common Station.

For a small byway the DVLR enjoyed a surprisingly long and remunerative life, but on 22 February 1965 the six miles south of Wheldrake were closed completely, just before the complete closure of the Market Weighton–Selby section of British Railways (see separate section). On 19 June 1968 the line was cut back to Elvington and again on 19 January 1973 to Dunnington. However, after the National Railway Museum opened in York in 1975 the remaining section of the DVLR was used to run steam-hauled trains for enthusiasts in the summer months. The normal motive power was the North Eastern–designed J72 0-6-0 tank engine 69023, which had acquired the name *Joem* in preservation, though more exotic engines, including the LNWR 2-4-0 *Hardwicke* put in appearances from time to time. The steam workings commenced in 1977 but ceased after 1979. By this time the only regular traffic over the line was grain from Dunnington and on 27 September 1981 the line closed completely.

Even so, the DVLR was not finished. The half-mile section west of Murton was within the land owned by the Yorkshire Museum of Farming at Murton Park. In 1985 the Light Railway Order for the line was transferred to the museum and the remaining line was reopened as a heritage line in 1993. The section to the east of Murton into York – and along the route of the Foss Island branch – has been converted into a cycle and walking track operated by Sustrans.

Royal Oak Junctions — Filey Holiday Camp

Passenger service withdrawn 17 July 1977
Distance ¾ mile
Company London & North Eastern Railway

Station closed *Date of closure*
Filey Holiday Camp 17 July 1977

In 1938 the government passed the Holidays with Pay Act, a measure which, as the title suggests, allowed workers to be granted annual holidays without forfeiting their regular wages over the period of their absence from work. Though now taken for granted, holidays with pay were a great advance for the majority of workers who previously would either not have been able to have holidays from work at all, or, if they could have afforded to be away from work might have found it difficult to pay for accommodation away from home. Day excursions had, of course, existed for a century before holidays with pay, but now it became possible for people of even modest means to go away for a week, or if very fortunate, a fortnight.

Growth in demand for time away prompted the development of a new form of holiday provision, the holiday camp, and the pioneer of the concept was the former showman Billy Butlin. His first holiday camp had opened at Skegness in 1936 and offered a week's stay, inclusive of three meals a day and all entertainment, from 35/- (£1.75) a week. Though suspended for the duration of the Second World War, Butlin's opened a number of new camps after hostilities ended, including one at Filey in 1947. Since holidaymakers were dependent on public transport the LNER constructed a short branch to the camp from the Driffield–Scarborough line between Hunmanby and Filey. The line began at a triangular junction at Royal Oak, allowing direct running from north and south. Along with one at the camp itself, the line had two signal boxes, the junction being controlled by a north and south box.

The station comprised two long island platforms, giving four platform faces in all, and was clearly not a place where anyone was expected to linger, having no buildings, only ticket collectors' cabins at the exits. Campers were taken to the camp on a 'road train' running in a subway, reflecting the ethos of 'organised leisure' which was the Butlin's hallmark. The line and station were mainly operational on Saturdays in the summer holiday season, then considerably shorter than now and mainly confined to the weeks from late July to early September. On summer Saturdays during the 1950s and early 1960s, however, the traffic could be heavy as this was the heyday of holiday camps before cheap air travel lured the British away to the fleshpots of southern Spain. In such busy times the operating staff on the line might be stretched and in 1956 an empty coaching stock train from Bridlington ran away because the fireman had forgotten to couple up the vacuum brake hoses between tender and train and in consequence the automatic brake was inoperative. The guard and driver had failed to test the brake before starting; had they done so the omission could not have gone unnoticed. K3 class 2-6-0 No. 61846 demolished the concrete stop-block at the end of one of the platforms and, though damaging itself in the process, caused no serious injuries.

With changing holiday patterns, Butlin's closed the Filey camp thirty years after opening, the station officially closing from 26 November 1977. Today the camp buildings have gone, but the station platforms remain.

Selby — Driffield

Passenger service withdrawn	20 September 1954 (but see text)	*Stations closed*	*Date of closure*
Distance	31 miles	Foggathorpe	20 September 1954
Company	Selby–Market Weighton: York & North Midland Railway	Holme *	20 September 1954
	Market Weighton–Driffield: Scarborough, Bridlington	Everingham	20 September 1954
	& West Riding Junction Railway	Market Weighton	29 November 1965
		Enthorpe	20 September 1954
Stations closed	*Date of closure*	Middleton-on-the-Wolds	20 September 1954
Cliff Common	20 September 1954	Bainton	20 September 1954
Menthorpe Gate	7 December 1953	Southburn	20 September 1954
Bubwith	20 September 1954		
High Field	20 September 1954		

* Also noted in some timetables as Holme Moor.

Cliff Common Station, 14 May 1953.

Even though there was a supposition that railway companies would compete with one another, the reality was that each tried to secure for itself a distinct territory in which, even if it was not the only operator, it was certainly the dominant one. The York & North Midland saw east Yorkshire naturally falling into its domain and was thus keen to promote a line across it from Selby northeastwards to Market Weighton, where it would make a junction with the line already promoted from York (see the section on Beverley–York). Authorised by an Act of 18 June 1846, the seventeen-mile route was relatively easy to construct and opened on 1 August 1848. Market Weighton thus became the terminus of a second line within two years but the decline in railway promotion after the collapse of the 'Railway Mania' of the mid 1840s ensured it remained so for almost twenty years until the opening of the line onwards to Beverley.

Selby — Driffield

Everingham Station, c.1905.

During the 1880s renewed interest in promoting new lines in east Yorkshire seems to have accompanied the authorisation of the Hull & Barnsley route from Cudworth to Hull. One such was the Scarborough & East Riding Junction Railway, which in 1884 produced a scheme for a route from Driffield to Market Weighton, thence striking off southwestwards to make a connection with the Hull & Barnsley at Howden. The parliamentary bill for this line failed, but in the following year the Scarborough, Bridlington & West Riding Junction Railway sought to revive elements of the previous scheme.

Selby — Driffield

Market Weighton Station, 31 August 1956.

The North Eastern, seeing that accommodation of the new proposals might be better than outright opposition, supported the plan for the construction of two sections, one between Cayton and Nafferton curiously bypassing Bridlington, and also between Driffield and Market Weighton. Passenger traffic began from 1 May 1890, goods having started a fortnight before; the North Eastern doubled the line south of Market Weighton, it having originally been single track, and worked the new route from the outset. The idea of linking the SB&WRJR to the Hull & Barnsley had not yet been forgotten and the independent company applied for parliamentary consent for a further extension to Wallingfen, and to the North Eastern at Staddlethorpe, three years later; however, Parliament declined to authorise either. The Scarborough company was formally absorbed by the North Eastern in 1913.

Selby — Driffield

Enthorpe Station, 2 June 1956.

In contrast to the Selby–Market Weighton section, the new line was more heavily engineered, traversing the chalk of the Wolds in a deep cutting near Enthorpe, reminiscent of the Hull & Barnsley's earthwork at Little Weighton.

Selby — Driffield

Bainton Station, *c.*1905.

The popularity of Bridlington, Filey and Scarborough as holiday destinations ensured the through route carried a considerable volume of excursions in summer, but the locally generated traffic was more modest. The LNER's last summer timetable showed only three return journeys a day, half as many as forty years before, with two through trains from Leeds to Bridlington on Saturdays. Unsurprisingly, the intermediate stations were closed in 1954, though a Selby–Driffield through passenger service of two trains a day, along with goods and excursion workings, continued until final closure in June 1965.

Stations closed on lines still open to passengers
Doncaster — York (East Coast main line)

Stations closed	Date
Riccall	15 September 1958
Escrick	8 June 1953
Naburn	8 June 1953

Escrick Station.

Naburn Station.

Doncaster — York (East Coast main line)

Hull — Scarborough *

Stations closed	Date	Stations closed	Date
Lockington	13 June 1960	Gristhorpe	16 February 1959
Lowthorpe	5 January 1970	Cayton	5 May 1952
Burton Agnes	5 January 1970		
Flamborough	5 January 1970	* Closed passenger stations on this line that were in the North Riding were
Carnaby	5 January 1970	Gristhorpe and Cayton.
Speeton	5 January 1970	

Lockington Station, *c.*1904.

Burton Agnes Station.

Gristhorpe Station, *c.*1910.

Hull — Scarborough